Grandma's List

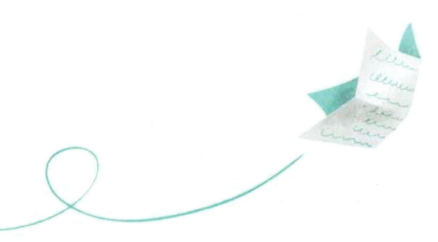

PORTIA DERY is a Ghanaian writer based in Tamale. She is an activist for literacy in Africa. Portia is the founder and current director of AYWO, the African Youth Writers Organization. *Grandma's List* is her first book.

TOBY NEWSOME is a South African illustrator based in Cape Town. He works in publishing and advertising for clients around the world. Toby has a special passion for narrative illustration and loves making a great story come to life on the page.

THE GOLDEN BAOBAB PRIZE is a set of prestigious awards that recognize outstanding African writers and illustrators of children's literature. Established in 2008, the goal of the prize is to inspire the creation of more children's stories from Africa, written by Africans.

First published in Ghana in 2016 by African Bureau Stories Ltd.
P.O. Box YK 822, Kanda, Greater Accra, Ghana
hello@africanbureau.com | www.africanbureau.com
Telephone: +233 55 870 3417

ISBN: 978 9988 9152 0 9

This paperback edition is published in Ghana in 2021 by African Bureau Stories Ltd. African Bureau Stories and associated logos are trademarks and/or registered trademarks of African Bureau Stories Ltd.

Text © Portia Dery, 2016
Cover and inside illustrations © Toby Newsome, 2016
Portia Dery and Toby Newsome assert the moral right to be identified as the author and illustrator respectively of this work.

All rights reserved
Also available as an ebook

This book is sold subject to the condition that it shall not, by way of trade or otherwise, be lent, hired out or otherwise circulated in any form of binding or cover other than that in which it is published. No part of this publication may be reproduced, stored in a retrieval system, or transmitted in any form or by any means (electronic, mechanical, photocopying, recording or otherwise) without the prior written permission of African Bureau Stories Ltd.

Grandma's List

Written by Portia Dery
Illustrated by Toby Newsome

GOLDEN BAOBAB PRIZE WINNER

Fatima was determined to save the day. She was tired of people treating her like a child. "I know what to do," she said to herself. **"I will save the day and be a superwoman."**

Just then, Grandma Eva appeared with her list of things to do; she looked overwhelmed and tired. She stretched her hands in the air and sighed. "How I wish God would send an angel to help me."

This was the golden opportunity Fatima had been waiting for. She knew exactly what to do. She ran up to Grandma and she said, "Hey Granny, I can help you with that list!"

"You?" exclaimed Grandma. "But you're too small."

"I am taller than most of my friends," answered Fatima.

"But there are a lot of things on that list, and you're only eight."

"Eight an' A HALF, Grandma!"

Fatima was fed up of everyone in the family thinking she was still a child. She was never considered when it came to serious work in the house.

"I said, I can!" replied Fatima. "Look here, I can read everything on your list!" she went on, grabbing the list from Grandma's hand.

"Okay, let's see then."

In a loud, excited voice Fatima read.

"Do you really understand everything on that list?" Grandma asked, looking at her old watch. It was getting late; there was no hope of finding someone else to run the errands for her. She had an appointment in town and she still had to find a cab at the station.

"Of course, Grandma! Just say yes, please!" begged Fatima.

"Okay, darling. I am late and the errands shouldn't be too difficult for a smart girl like you. Be careful!"

"Thanks, Grandma!" Fatima beamed with joy.

"I will be back in no time!"

Fatima was excited. She ran all the way to the grocery shop without stopping. She didn't even stop when Helen and her friends invited her for a drink of Bissap. They shouted, **"Fatima, come and play with us!"**

She kept a straight face and said, "I am very busy today." She was determined to do everything on Grandma's list in time.

She didn't even stop to watch the children mould clay into toys, nor did she stop to beg the bigger boys for mangoes.

Fatima smiled when she thought how proud her mother would be when she heard how Fatima had saved the day.

"**Hello, Fati!**" Mr Henry the shopkeeper said. She hated the name Fati; it made her feel younger than her age.

"Hello sir, I have a few things to buy." She wore a serious look.

"Really? Let's see what you want, then." He smiled.

"I have the list here." She dipped her hand into her pocket. Deeper her hand went, but the list wasn't there. She quickly checked the other pocket but it was empty too. She turned her pockets inside out, but only the money Grandma had given her fell out.

"Is there a problem?" Mr Henry asked, concerned.

"I can't find Grandma's to-do list," answered Fatima.

"You can always come back later," Mr Henry suggested.

But there was no way Fatima would go back home without buying Grandma's things: that would be admitting that she was still a child who could not even run simple errands on a list.

"NO!"

"I remember everything on the list. I memorized it," claimed Fatima.

"Really? You're a smart girl, then. Tell me, what was on the list?"

"Hmm ... Grandma asked me to buy flour."

"Which type?" Mr Henry asked.

"Are there different types of flour?"

"Yes, dear."

"Cornflour."

"Are you sure?"

"Very certain, sir."

"Okay. And what else?"

"Sugar and a full chicken." She was excited. **"I remember very well now!"** Fatima was sure she was right.

"Here they are." Mr Henry handed her the cornflour, sugar and chicken. "Say hi to your grandma and the family."

"I will. Thank you, sir," she said, running out.

Fatima was happy. She had finished the first part of her errands very quickly, so she ran all the way back home. When she arrived, she was out of breath.

Agnes was in the yard, chatting with two friends. "Here is what Grandma asked me to buy for you," Fatima said, feeling very important. "And she says you should prepare palm nut soup with chicken."

"Okay," answered Agnes, distracted. She didn't bother to ask why Grandma suddenly preferred chicken instead of beef, nor to check the items. **"Put them in the kitchen!"** she said to Fatima.

Fatima didn't mind at all. She went straight into the kitchen and poured the sugar into an empty container and the cornflour into the baking flour bowl. Then she put the chicken in the fridge.

Uncle Dan was on the veranda playing with his phone. "Grandma says you should feed the goats and free the hens," she said. Uncle Dan was only twenty years old but Fatima had to call him "uncle" as if he was very old.

But Uncle Dan didn't look up, and he didn't bother to ask why the hens needed to be freed instead of the goats. Instead, he said, **"You do that!"**

Fatima didn't mind at all. She went straight to the back yard. She opened the door of the hens' coop, and the hens clucked and rushed out. Then she plucked some mango leaves from a branch that had been cut down and pushed it through the hole to feed the goats.

Finally she delivered her last message. "Grandpa, Grandma says you should plant the groundnuts in the garden today."

But Grandpa was busy listening to the radio. He scratched his head. **"Groundnuts?"** He didn't bother to ask why Grandma had suddenly changed her mind about sowing groundnuts instead of beans. He simply said, "Okay, I will."

Agnes had said goodbye to her friends and was preparing dinner. "When is Grandma coming back?" she asked from the kitchen.

"I hope she comes soon!" said Fatima, excited, on her way to the gate to be the first to see Grandma when she came back. She couldn't wait to tell her that she had finished all her errands.

Later in the evening, the whole family sat around the huge dining table to eat an early supper. Fatima knew this was her opportunity to tell everyone about her busy day.

"Fatima, are you alright?" her mother finally asked.

"Yes," she replied, casting a glance at her grandma. **"Grandma, tell them how I ran errands for you!"**

Grandma laughed and said, "We must eat first! Agnes, please could you serve the food."

Agnes dished out the palm nut soup with chicken and rice. Then Grandma's face dimmed. She stared at the food, looking surprised.

"I thought I asked you to prepare palm nut soup with beef," Grandma said, remembering it very well because she had written it on the list.

"Ooh! This soup tastes different," announced Grandpa.

"Oh my God!" Mother said.

"What is this?" Father asked.

"Goodness!"
Grandma exclaimed.

"The soup tastes like
... there is sugar in it!"
Uncle Dan stammered.

"**But how can that be?** I put in the salt myself." Agnes looked confused.

"Did you taste the food after putting in the salt?" asked Grandma.

Agnes shook her head violently. "But ... it was salt I put in the soup ... " Then she paused and she suddenly remembered.

"Fatima!"

"What has that got to do with me?" Fatima asked.

"Fati?" Grandma said. "Did you give Agnes sugar instead of salt?"

Then Fatima remembered. "But you asked me to buy sugar for Agnes."

"Me? Didn't I write salt on that list? Where is the list?"

"I kept it in my pocket but ... I lost it," confessed Fatima.

"Fati, if you lost the list how did you run the errands?" Her mother sounded alarmed.

"I memorized it ... well, I THOUGHT I did."

Fatima's heart pounded against her chest. Her dream of saving the day was becoming a nightmare.

"Fati!" Mother called.
"Fati!" Grandpa said.
"Faaati!" Father sighed.
"Fati!" Agnes shouted.
"FATI!" Uncle Dan called.

"**What else did you memorize from Grandma's list?**" Mother asked gently.

"Well … I freed the hens and fed the goats because Uncle Dan was playing with his phone."

"I poured the sugar into the empty container in the kitchen and the cornflour in the baking container, because Agnes was chatting with her friends."

"And I told Grandpa to plant groundnuts in the back yard too," she said.

Fatima had just realized the mistakes she might have made. She knew this was the end: now no one would listen to her talk about being a big girl. She was so sad that she wanted to run and hide in her room, but she knew she had to be brave and wait for her punishment.

But Grandma laughed and laughed and soon everyone joined in: Mother, Father, Uncle Dan, Grandpa and even Agnes. They laughed so hard that the dog started to bark.

"So I guess we have a cake made with cornflour," Mother said.

"Groundnuts planted instead of beans. And goats locked inside while the hens make merry," Father said.

"And special palm nut soup made with sugar!" Agnes laughed.

"Aren't you all annoyed with me?" Fatima asked with a puzzled look.

"Why should we?" said Grandma with a kind smile. "It wasn't only your fault." Then she looked at everybody and added, "If Agnes, Dan and Grandpa had paid attention and performed their duties, we wouldn't be eating sugared soup now!"

Fatima looked at her family and laughed. Perhaps it wasn't bad being a child after all ...

Printed in France by Amazon
Brétigny-sur-Orge, FR

14012737R00020